AF538510

DAY BY DAY WITH...

ELENA DELLE DONNE

BY
TAMMY GAGNE

PUBLISHERS
P.O. Box 196
Hockessin, Delaware 19707
Visit us on the web: www.mitchelllane.com
Comments? Email us:
mitchelllane@mitchelllane.com

Printing 1 2 3 4 5 6 7 8 9

RANDY'S CORNER

DAY BY DAY WITH...

Adam Jones
Alex Morgan
Beyoncé
Bindi Sue Irwin
Calvin Johnson
Carrie Underwood
Chloë Moretz
Dwayne "The Rock" Johnson
Elena Delle Donne
Eli Manning
Gabby Douglas
Justin Bieber
LeBron James
Manny Machado
Mia Hamm
Miley Cyrus
Missy Franklin
Selena Gomez
Shaun White
Stephen Hillenburg
Taylor Swift
Willow Smith

Library of Congress Cataloging-in-Publication Data
Gagne, Tammy.
Day by day with Elena Delle Donne / by Tammy Gagne.
pages cm. — (Randy's corner)
Includes bibliographical references and index.
ISBN 978-1-61228-634-1 (library bound)
1. Donne, Elena Delle. 2. Basketball players—United States—Biography. 3. Women basketball players—United States—Biography. I. Title.
GV884.D65G34 2014
796.323092—dc23
[B]

2014006937

eBook ISBN: 97816912286600

ABOUT THE AUTHOR: Tammy Gagne is the author of numerous books for adults and children, including *Day by Day with Missy Franklin* and *Mike Trout* for Mitchell Lane Publishers. She resides in northern New England with her husband and son. One of her favorite pastimes is visiting schools to speak to kids about the writing process.

PUBLISHER'S NOTE: The following story has been thoroughly researched and to the best of our knowledge represents a true story. While every possible effort has been made to ensure accuracy, the publisher will not assume liability for damages caused by inaccuracies in the data and makes no warranty on the accuracy of the information contained herein.

PBP

DAY BY DAY WITH

ELENA DELLE DONNE

The University of Delaware's women's basketball team was never one of the best. Not until 2012, anyway. The team, called the Fightin' Blue Hens, started winning more games than they ever had before. In November 2012, they were suddenly number eight in the *USA Today* Coaches Poll.

ELENA DELLE DONNE DRIBBLES PAST KENTUCKY WILDCATS GUARD JENNIFER O'NEILL.

The Fightin' Blue Hens ended their year with thirty-two wins and four losses. It was a school record—the team had never won so many games in one year. "It's pretty wild," University of Delaware student and basketball player Elena Delle Donne told *USA Today*.

IT'S THE SECOND HALF OF THE NCAA WOMEN'S BASKETBALL TOURNAMENT, AND A'DIA MATHIES TRIES TO PASS THE BALL TO ONE OF HER KENTUCKY WILDCATS TEAMMATES. BUT ELENA AND DELAWARE FIGHTIN' BLUE HENS GUARD LAUREN CARRA ARE RIGHT THERE TO STOP HER.

IT OFTEN SEEMS LIKE NOTHING CAN GET IN ELENA'S WAY. HERE, SHE SPRINGS INTO THE AIR DURING THE SECOND HALF OF THE NCAA TOURNAMENT EAST REGION SWEET 16 GAME IN BRIDGEPORT, CONNECTICUT. SHE TAKES HER SHOT OVER KENTUCKY'S SAMARIE WALKER.

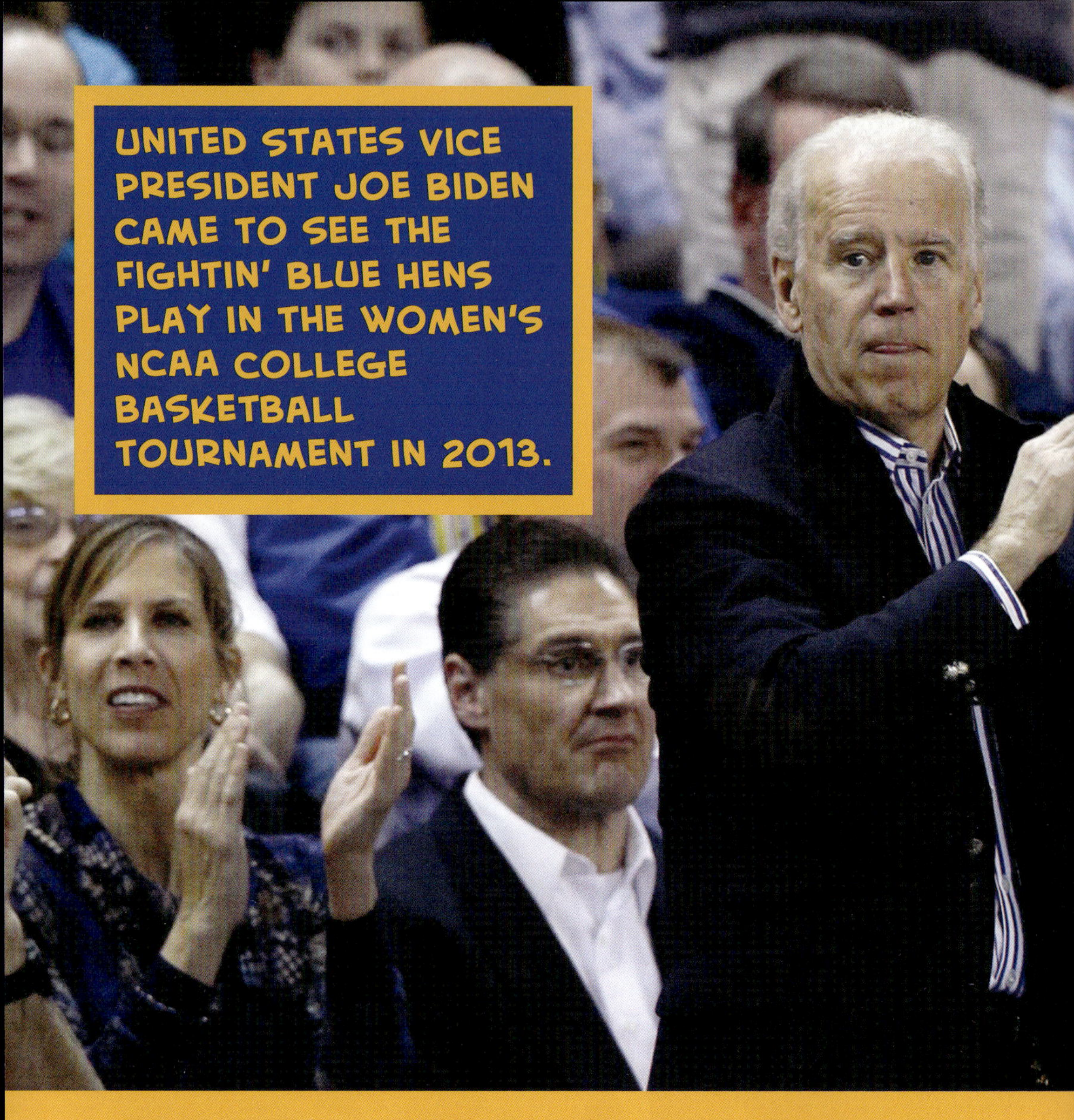

UNITED STATES VICE PRESIDENT JOE BIDEN CAME TO SEE THE FIGHTIN' BLUE HENS PLAY IN THE WOMEN'S NCAA COLLEGE BASKETBALL TOURNAMENT IN 2013.

United States Vice President Joe Biden also went to the University of Delaware. He wanted to watch the team play their last game of the year. But as vice president, Biden had to do important things that day. So he called the Fightin' Blue Hens' coach

Tina Martin. He said that he was sorry he couldn't be there. According to *USA Today* Elena said, "Okay, Coach, you have the vice president calling your cell phone. That's kind of big-time now."

ELENA'S HIGH SCHOOL DAYS

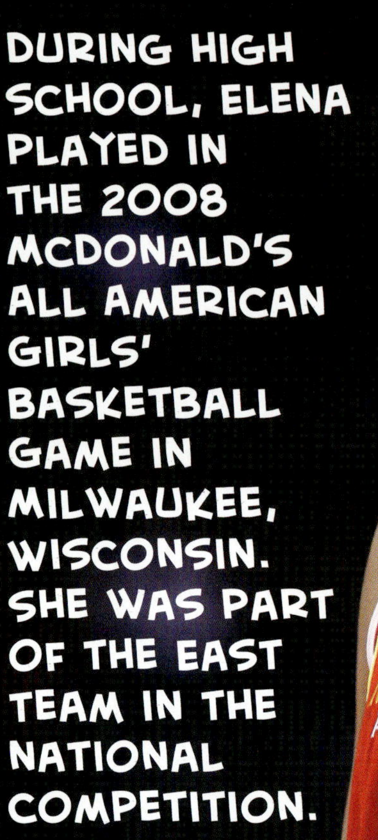

DURING HIGH SCHOOL, ELENA PLAYED IN THE 2008 MCDONALD'S ALL AMERICAN GIRLS' BASKETBALL GAME IN MILWAUKEE, WISCONSIN. SHE WAS PART OF THE EAST TEAM IN THE NATIONAL COMPETITION.

Although Elena was from Wilmington, Delaware, the first college she picked wasn't in her home state. Instead, she had decided to go to the University of Connecticut. After two days at the school, though, she realized that Delaware was where she wanted to be after all.

BEFORE ELENA EVEN STARTED COLLEGE, SHE PLAYED FOR TEAM USA.

IN 2011, THE UNITED STATES CLAIMED THE TITLE AT THE 26TH SUMMER UNIVERSIADE WOMEN'S BASKETBALL TOURNAMENT IN SHENZHEN, CHINA. THE US DEFEATED CHINESE TAIPEI WITH A FINAL SCORE OF 101 TO 66 IN THE FINAL GAME. HERE, ELENA DELLE DONNE IS SEEN BREAKING THROUGH HUANG PING-JEN'S DEFENSE.

ELENA IS A POWERFUL GUARD. SHE IS SEEN HERE BLOCKING A SHOT BY MARYLAND TERRAPINS PLAYER ALICIA DEVAUGHN AT THE COMCAST CENTER IN COLLEGE PARK, MARYLAND, IN 2011.

Some people thought that Elena had made the wrong choice. After all, the University of Connecticut was a top team. She could have done great things there. But she wanted to be closer to her family—one very special family member in particular.

THE UNIVERSITY OF CONNECTICUT HUSKIES TAKE A PHOTO WITH THEIR 2013 NCAA TROPHY.

ELENA AND HER FAMILY—BROTHER GENE, MOTHER JOAN, SISTER LIZZIE, AND FATHER ERNIE—POSE FOR A PHOTO WITH HER COACH TINA MARTIN.

From the time Elena's older sister Lizzie was born, she couldn't see or hear. "Skype, cell phone, texting, email—doesn't work with Liz," Elena told ABC News. "We've never

spoken a word to one another. . . . She knows me by my smell and my feel. . . . So when I did leave, I lost Lizzie basically. Well, she lost me and I wasn't okay with that."

ELENA WITH UNIVERSITY OF DELAWARE VOLLEYBALL COACH BONNIE KENNY

At first it looked like Elena might quit basketball for good. After enrolling at the University of Delaware, she learned that she was good at volleyball. Her family was happy for her. But they thought basketball would be a better choice.

TOLEDO CENTER YOLANDA RICHARDSON AND ELENA BATTLE FOR REBOUNDING POSITION IN THE FIRST ROUND GAME OF THE 2011 WOMEN'S NATIONAL INVITATIONAL TOURNAMENT.

Elena's family loves sports as much as she does. Her father Ernie played golf and basketball at Columbia University. And her mother, Joan, was a swimmer in high school.

Elena's brother Gene played football for Duke and Middle Tennessee.

ELENA GOT TO THROW OUT THE FIRST PITCH AT A CHICAGO CUBS BASEBALL GAME.

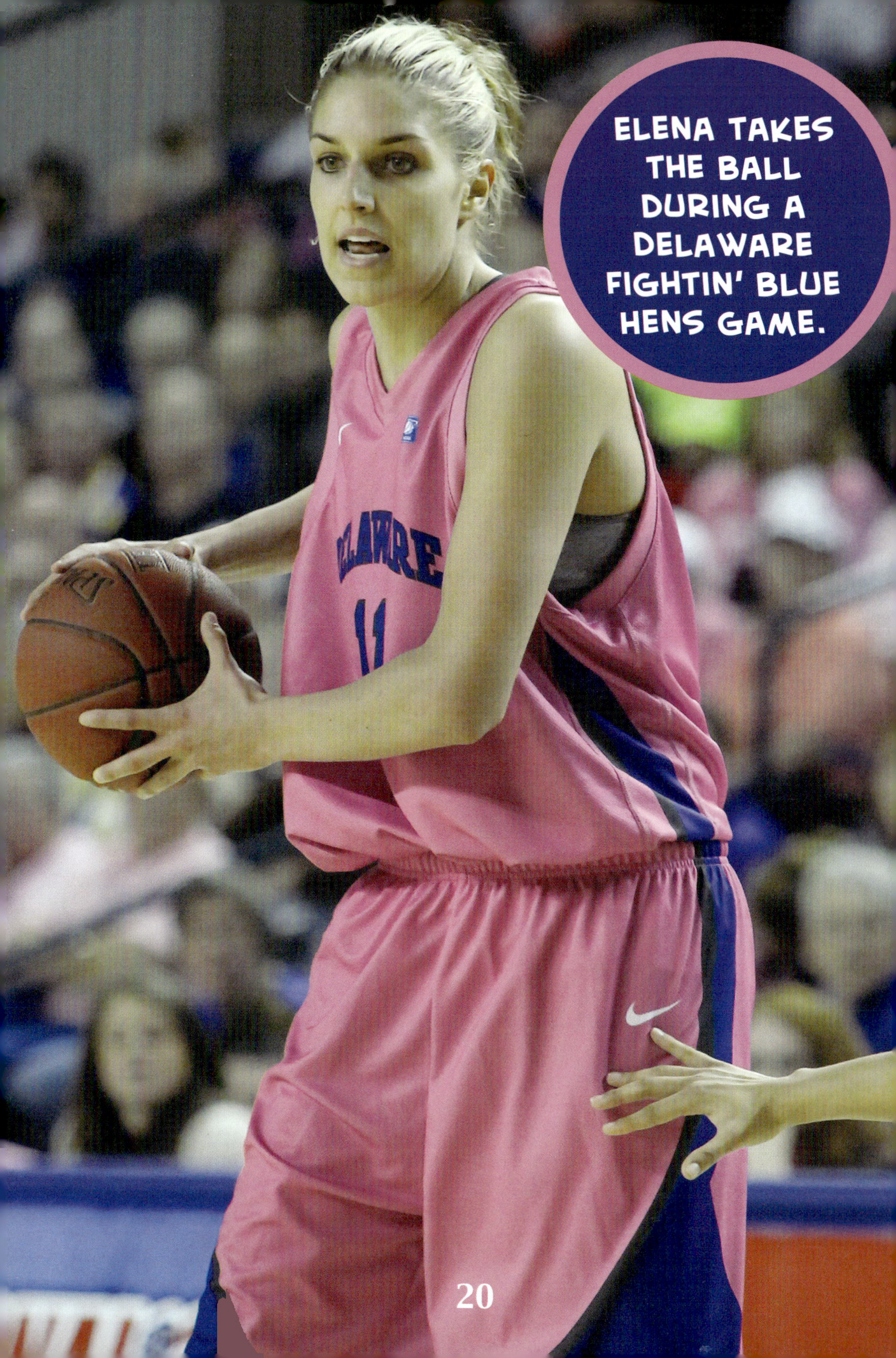
ELENA TAKES THE BALL DURING A DELAWARE FIGHTIN' BLUE HENS GAME.

Elena wasn't going to give up basketball. She just needed a break. "I love everything that is involved in this sport," she told ABC News. "And when I stopped enjoying it, I stepped away from the game. . . . Now I play it for the passion and love of the game." Clearly, her plan worked.

IN 2013, ELENA BECAME THE NINTH PLAYER IN WOMEN'S COLLEGE BASKETBALL HISTORY TO SCORE 3,000 POINTS. HER FANS CHEERED HER ON WITH SIGNS AND POM-POMS.

The Fightin' Blue Hens won an NCAA tournament game in 2012, a first for the school. They beat the University of Arkansas with a final score of 73 to 42. Elena scored 39 of those points—nearly as many points as the entire other team! She averaged 27.5 points per game that year. That was more points than any women's college basketball player in the United States.

The University of Delaware Fightin' Blue Hens huddle before a game

In 2013, Elena became the second Delaware player in history to be drafted by the Women's National Basketball Association (WNBA). She was the second pick, after Brittney Griner. Elena would now be part of the Chicago Sky WNBA team.

FIRST PICK
BRITTNEY
GRINER
SECOND
PICK
ELENA
DELLE
DONNE
THIRD
PICK
SKYLAR
DIGGINS

It looked like the Sky had made the right choice. In her rookie year, or her first season with the team, she averaged 18.1 points. The Sky made the WNBA playoffs for the first time. In September 2013, Elena was named WNBA Rookie of the Year. There were a lot of good rookie players that year, so Elena was excited when she received the award.

IT WAS JUST A REGULAR SEASON GAME BETWEEN THE CHICAGO SKY AND THE WASHINGTON MYSTICS. BUT ELENA ALWAYS GIVES HER ALL ON THE COURT. HERE, SHE SHOOTS THE BALL OVER MYSTICS CENTER EMMA MEESSEMAN.

IN 2013 ELENA WAS NAMED WNBA ROOKIE OF THE YEAR.

It's very important to Elena to help others, too. In November 2013, she visited a high school near Chicago to coach Special Olympics basketball players. In Special Olympics, people who have trouble with skills

ELENA WORKS WITH KIDS DURING A BASKETBALL CLINIC AT LOYOLA UNIVERSITY IN CHICAGO.

like thinking and learning get to play sports. "I love working with the Special Olympics," Elena told the *Glencoe News*. "It's a really great experience seeing their joy as they play the game with others."

Elena tells her fans to follow their hearts. "When I made a decision to not go to [the University of] Connecticut, it was very tough but I was true to myself," she told *Vibe Vixen*. "It really did make me stronger and that's really my message. Follow your heart, know what your passions are, and if you're passionate, you can do whatever you set your mind to."

IN 2014 ELENA WAS NAMED A SPECIAL OLYMPICS GLOBAL AMBASSADOR. SHE IS SEEN HERE TAKING PART IN THE UNIFY BASKETBALL CLINIC AT HOMEWOOD FLOSSMOOR HIGH SCHOOL.

FURTHER READING

FIND OUT MORE

Diehl, David. *Slam Dunk!* Asheville, NC: Lark Books, 2008.

Gibbons, Gail. *My Basketball Book.* New York: HarperCollins, 2000.

McClellan, Ray. *Basketball.* Minneapolis, MN: Bellwether Media, 2009.

WORKS CONSULTED

ESPN W. "Elena Delle Donne Named Top Rookie." September 20, 2013. http://espn.go.com/wnba/story/_/id/9696595/chicago-sky-elena-delle-donne-named-wnba-rookie-year

Longman, Jeré. "At Pinnacle, Stepping Away From Basketball." *New York Times*, October 18, 2008. http://www.nytimes.com/2008/10/19/sports/ncaabasketball/19athlete.html?pagewanted=all&_r=0

Ludka, Alexandra. "Why a Rising Women's Basketball Star Left Hoops Heaven for the Home Team." ABC News, March 20, 2012. http://abcnews.go.com/blogs/lifestyle/2012/03/why-a-rising-womens-basketball-star-left-hoops-heaven-for-the-home-team/

Platon, Adelle. "Vixen TV: Elena Delle Donne Discusses Her Future in the WNBA." *Vibe Vixen*, April 23, 2013. http://www.vibevixen.com/2013/04/vixen-tv-elena-delle-donne-discusses-her-future-in-the-wnba/

Schering, Steve. "Chicago Sky's Delle Donne Visits New Trier's Special Olympians." *Glencoe News*, December 23, 2013. http://glencoe.suntimes.com/news/donne-WTK-11212013:article

Schilken, Chuck. "Brittney Griner, Elena Delle Donne are Picked 1-2 in WNBA Draft." *Los Angeles Times*, April 16, 2013. http://articles.latimes.com/2013/apr/16/sports/la-sp-sn-elena-delle-donne-20130416

Whiteside, Kelly. "Elena Delle Donne, Delaware Making History." *USA Today*, March 8, 2012. http://usatoday30.usatoday.com/sports/college/womensbasketball/story/2012-03-05/elena-delle-done-lifts-delaware-to-new-heights/53420806/1

ON THE INTERNET

Chicago Sky Website
http://www.wnba.com/sky/

ESPN W: "Get to Know: Elena Delle Donne"
http://espn.go.com/espnw/athletes-life/blog/post/9403/elena-delle-donne

SIKids.com: "Griner, Delle Donne, and Diggins Talk with Our Kid Reporter"
http://www.sikids.com/sikidstv/griner-delle-donne-and-diggins-talk-with-our-kid-reporter?page=1

USA Basketball: "Elena Delle Donne"
http://www.usab.com/bios/delle-donne_elena.html

INDEX

PHOTO CREDITS: Cover, p. 3—Anthony Nesmith/Cal Sport Media/Newscom; pp. 4–5, 6—Bill Shettle/Cal Sport Media/Newscom; p. 7—John Woike/MCT/Newscom; pp. 8–9—AP Photo/Patrick Semansky; p. 9—Dannykuconn/cc-by-sa; p. 10—Ben Smidt/Icon SMI 295/Newscom; p. 11—Meng Yongmin Xinhua News Agency/Newscom; p. 12—G Flume/Maryland Terrapins/Getty Images; p. 13—Stacy Revere/Getty Images; pp. 14, 16, 25—Courtesy of Delle Donne family; pp. 14–15, 20, 21—Saquan Stimpson/ZUMA Press/Newscom; p. 17—Scott Grau/ZUMAPRESS/Newscom; p. 18—AP Photo/Dick Druckman; p. 19—Warren Wimmer/CSR/Icon SMI 484/Warren Chicago Sports Review Magazine/Newscom; pp. 22–23—AP Photo/Saquan Stimpson; p. 26—Daniel Kucin Jr/Icon SMI DAW/Newscom; p. 27—AP Photo/Nam Y. Huh; pp. 28–29—AP Photo/Paul Beaty; pp. 30–31—Barry Brecheisen/Invision for Special Olympics, Inc/AP Images.